Texts from Mittens

Texts from Mittens

A Cat Who Has an Unlimited Data Plan… and Isn't Afraid to Use It

Texts from Mittens:
A Cat Who Has an Unlimited Data Plan...
and Isn't Afraid to Use it

ISBN-13: 978-0-373-89322-5

Library of Congress Cataloging-in-Publication Data
Bailey, Angie.
  Texts from Mittens : a cat who has an unlimited data plan-and isn't afraid to use it / Angie Bailey.
     pages cm
  ISBN 978-0-373-89322-5 (alk. paper)
1. Cats--Humor. I. Title.
  PN6231.C23B34 2015
  818'.5402--dc23
                         2014031304

www.Harlequin.com

Printed in China.

MITTENS

"Mittens' texts are extremely witty, cutting and hilariously blunt."
~Francesco Marciuliano, Author of *I Could Pee on This: And Other Poems by Cats*

"Mittens is a gift to brighten your day!"
~Kate Benjamin, Hauspanther founder and Co-Author of *Catification* with Jackson Galaxy

"Texts from Mittens makes me wish my cat had thumbs!"
~Jeremy Greenberg, Author of *Sorry I Barfed on Your Bed*

"Mittens' sardonic quips take cat attitude to a whole new level!"
~Susan Michals, Curator of Cat Art Show Los Angeles

  SEND

CHARACTER GUIDE

Mittens:
A text-happy, indoor tuxie who loves *Judge Judy,* liver treats, fancy drinking fountains and creating unnecessary drama.

Mom:
A single, working woman who loves puns and dabbles in online dating. She (usually) sees through Mittens' schemes and supplies the treats.

Phil:
The Lab-mix "filthy hound" who lives with Mittens and Mom. He constantly irritates Mittens just by "being Phil."

Stumpy:
Mittens' wild best friend who lives down the block. A large, indoor-outdoor, orange tabby who visits Mittens to watch TV, eat treats and enjoy (lots of) catnip.

Grandma:
The bearer of fancy food and presents. Mittens makes special allowances for Grandma when it comes to taking photos, wearing costumes and participating in other degrading activities.

Drunk Patty:
The usually tipsy, tacky, next-door neighbor who adores Mittens and feeds him and Phil when Mom is gone. Mittens is annoyed by everything that is Drunk Patty.

1

3

MITTENS

Why does Phil turn around in circles before he lies down?

I don't know. Dogs just do that sometimes.

He looks ridiculous. This is the animal you call a "watch dog"? I'd do a better job.

Mitty, you hide when the doorbell rings.

I prefer to think of it as "hidden surveillance."

SEND

MITTENS

Drunk Patty came over and fell asleep on my cat tree!

Let her sleep it off.

Where am I supposed to hang out?

Sofa?

It's utter pandemonium here and you don't care!

SEND

4

If I have to hear "Dancing Queen" one more time, I'm going to drown myself in my fancy drinking fountain.

If you hadn't chewed through my ear bud wires, you wouldn't have to.

Don't blame me for your poor taste in music.

FIVE pairs of ear buds.

Stop deflecting.

SEND

Why can't I come to the party with you?

It's for humans, Mitty.

It's a cruel joke.

What?

Being born in a tuxedo and never getting to go anywhere fancy.

SEND

6

8

9

11

14

18

FURIZON 3G 10:30 AM

MITTENS

Phil drooled all over Mr. Fuzzy!

I'll wash your blanket tonight.

But I can't knead on him when he's wet!

I'll be home soon.

I can't wait!

You're awfully kneady, Mittens. LOL!

You're a horrible person.

SEND

FURIZON 3G 10:10 AM

MITTENS

I like your new pillow.

I know you do. You totally hijacked it last night.

We shared!

Shared? You took 99% of the pillow!

Poor you and your fancy pillow. I'll sleep on the hard linoleum tonight.

Martyr.

#PillowTyrant

SEND

19

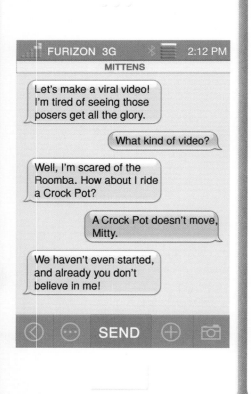

MITTENS

Let's make a viral video! I'm tired of seeing those posers get all the glory.

What kind of video?

Well, I'm scared of the Roomba. How about I ride a Crock Pot?

A Crock Pot doesn't move, Mitty.

We haven't even started, and already you don't believe in me!

    SEND   ⊕   📷

MITTENS

Phil's breath is horrific!

He's a dog.

I demand you bring home a little hazmat suit for me.

See you tonight, Mitty.

I'll be the one thrashing about on the floor, gasping for fresh air.

    SEND   ⊕   📷

21

24

25

26

28

29

31

33

MITTENS

FYI: I won't be wearing that pirate Halloween costume I saw in the bag.

C'mon, Mitty. Just for a few photos? Please?

As long as it's quick and I don't have to see any of the pics.

Fine. I even have a little eye patch for your eye!

How about patches for both eyes?

SEND

MITTENS

Mittens, where are you?

Why?

My water glass is tipped over.

What? The dog is automatically innocent?

He's outside. This has cat written all over it.

Mother! I feel profiled! I'm ashamed of you!

SEND

35

36

37

FURIZON 3G   2:50 PM

MITTENS

Someone stole my blanket!

Grandma accidentally packed it when she was over yesterday.

Aghast! Grandma kidnapped Mr. Fuzzy!

She'll bring it back.

You're awfully nonchalant about your rapscallion of a mother.

⊙ ⋯ SEND ⊕ ▢

FURIZON 3G   9:02 AM

MITTENS

What's wrong with the computer?

You contracted a virus from the Judge Judy message board.

Judy gave me a virus??

Not exactly.

I should go to the vet for some Clavamox. I feel ashamed!

⊙ ⋯ SEND ⊕ ▢

38

39

41

43

What was that thing you were wearing this morning?

A pedometer. It counts my steps. I need to move around more often.

Cool. I want one.

You probably should get more exercise.

You probably should mind your own business.

SEND

Get off the counter.

It's an act of civil disobedience because you won't buy me the new liver treats!

You have tons of old ones.

Tyranny!

SEND

44

46

47

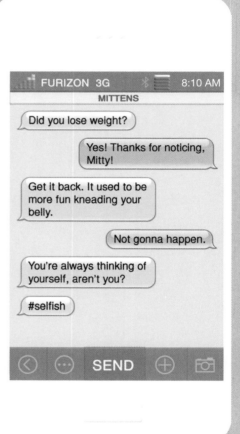

48

49

What happened to those pants I've been napping on?

In the wash. I'm going to wear them this weekend.

You moved them? I was using them!

They're MY pants.

Listen here, Sisterhood of the Traveling Pants, I expect them wadded up, back on the bed by 7 tonight.

SEND

Why are there no cat parks? Phil gets to go to the dog park. No fair.

Cats might freak out in strange surroundings.

You mean like the VET? You have no trouble dropping me off there.

Not the same thing.

Need a helmet for that back-pedaling?

SEND

53

55

56

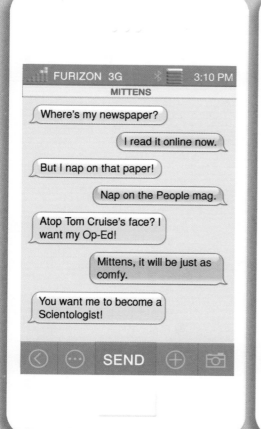

FURIZON 3G
6:45 AM
MITTENS
Why are you cursing?
You were chewing on my boot laces again! They're soaking wet!
I can't indulge now and again?
Ick! Now I have to wear something else.
Um, I wouldn't wear your sneakers either.
Mitty!
SEND

FURIZON 3G
3:10 PM
MITTENS
Who's this Easter Bunny?
He visits our house on Easter Eve and fills your baskets with lots of treats.
A giant rabbit sneaks in while I'm sleeping?
Yes.
That's alarming!
Why do we not have a panic room?
SEND

61

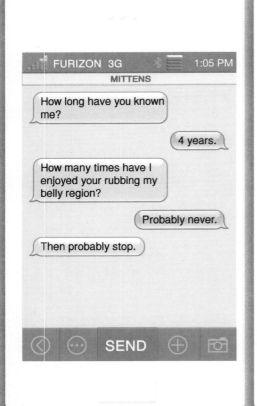

FURIZON 3G 2:15 PM
MITTENS

Please remove the photo of me in the gnome costume from Facebook.

It's cute!

I'll post the booze cruise pic of you. Password?

No way.

What's your mother's maiden name?

Carlson. Why?

Dammit.

SEND

FURIZON 3G 3:23 PM
MITTENS

Where's my felt rhino?

Oh, I found it in my purse.

You were trying to steal my toy!

I think you dropped it in there.

Crook! Scoundrel!

Bye, Mittens.

Enjoy the spoils of your thievery.

SEND

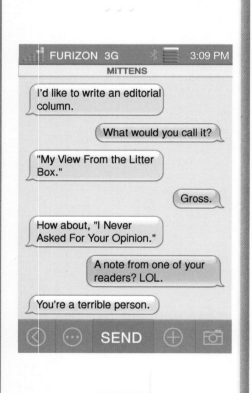

64

65

67

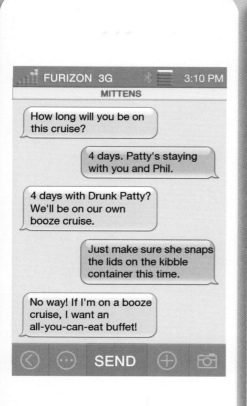

69

FURIZON 3G 11:24 AM

MITTENS

Come home.

Why?

You need to change the filter on my fancy drinking fountain.

I just changed it.

So?

I'll look at it later.

Fine. Anyway, I hear dehydration is the new look this season.

SEND

FURIZON 3G 2:10 PM

MITTENS

Grandma dropped off some litter.

It's non-clumping CLAY litter. So 1979.

We'll use it til it's gone. Retro is in fashion.

Great. Grab a Tab cola, turn on The Love Boat, and I'll be right back.

After I relieve myself in my CLAY, NON-CLUMPING LITTER.

SEND

71

74

76

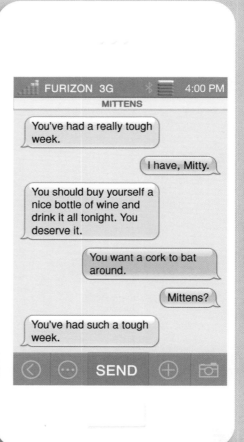

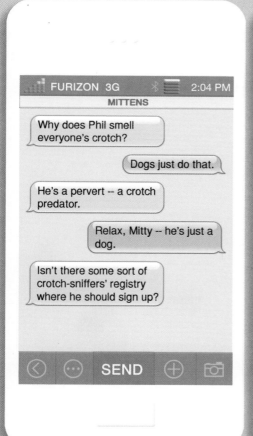

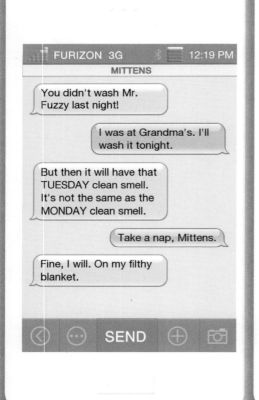

86

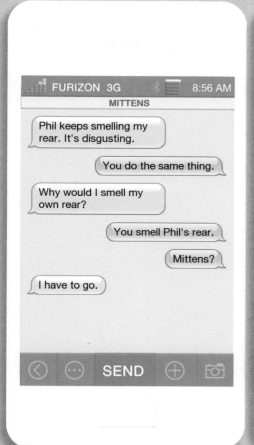

Phil keeps smelling my rear. It's disgusting.

You do the same thing.

Why would I smell my own rear?

You smell Phil's rear.

Mittens?

I have to go.

Mitty, I saw the book you're reading.

What book?

The one you're hiding under your cat bed.

What of it?

You know it's not really about how to kill a mockingbird.

I thought it was moving slowly.

87

89

90

91

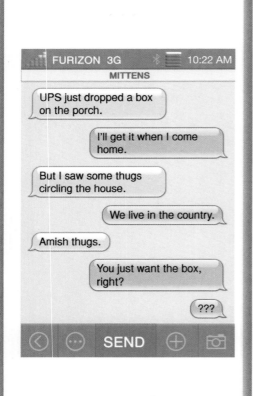

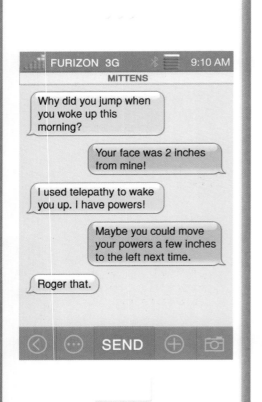

94

95

97

99

MITTENS

For Christmas, I'd like a top hat.

You don't like hats.

I want to look fancy.

And how about silver cufflinks?

You don't have anything with cuffs, Mittens.

Inconsequential!

SEND

MITTENS

Phil's snoring. I can't sleep.

Poke him a little. He'll stop.

Are you sure? I don't know about that.

Do you want to snuggle in bed with me?

Yes.

I love you, Mitty.

I love you too, Mama.

SEND

CREDITS

Kari, Darrell and Drake Osment: pages vi, 7, 10, 17, 22, 35, 38, 44, 45, 59, 66, 67, 77

Angie Bailey: pages vi, vii, 24, 28, 49, 78, 83, 84, 91, 93

Katy Herman: pages vi, vii, 4, 20, 36, 51, 68

Kari Achenbach: page vii, 13

Marina Dickey: page 2

Toni Nicholson: page 74

Hank Elzweig: page 58

The following images originally appeared on Catster.com: pages 1ab, 6ab, 7b, 9ab, 11ab, 12ab, 13a, 15ab, 17b, 18a, 21a, 25b, 26a, 29a, 31ab, 32b, 34b, 47a, 50b, 53b, 57a, 60b, 61a, 63a, 65ab, 69b, 70a, 73b, 74ab, 78a, 79a, 81b, 85b, 89a, 90b, 92ab, 97b

ACKNOWLEDGMENTS

Texts from Mittens wouldn't have been possible without the ongoing support of my friends at Catster.com, from where the column originated. Endless gratitude to you for taking a chance on Mitty!

Much gratitude to the *Texts from Mittens* online readers, whose love of a neurotic feline character and his wacky world make my heart sing. I love laughing with you every day!

Thank you to Jay Harris and his wild creativity skills for creating the initial Mittens digital image.

A lot of this craziness wouldn't have been possible without the ongoing collaboration of Katy Herman, Kari Achenbach, and Kari, Darrell and Drake Osment: Your patience and willingness to set up and take endless (sometimes strange) photos is golden. And of course, lots of ear-scritches and head-butts to Bullet, Ivan and Bombur.

Thanks to Becca Hunt, my cat-crazy editor at Harlequin. You made the entire experience so extraordinarily fun and delightfully seamless. Thanks to Fiona Cunningham, whose contagious enthusiasm makes her the perfect digital marketing manager for Mittens.

Once again, my agent Sorche Fairbank of Fairbank Literary Representation and I teamed up to share ridiculous cat humor with the world. You continue to be the most fantastic partner any cat-loving writer could hope for, and the best agent *ever*! Not even kidding.

And, of course, thank you to my friends and family (human and feline), who constantly encourage me, love me and allow me to immerse myself in the world of Mittens. John, your patience and willingness to act excited about silly cat stuff (even when it's maybe not that exciting) is award-worthy. You get some sort of husband award. I love you.